WORLD DANCES

LET'S DANCE

Tracy M. Maurer

The Rourke Press, Inc.
Vero Beach, Florida 32964

Tracy M. Maurer, author of the Dance Series, specializes in non-fiction and business writing. She has previously worked with several educational organizations on various writing projects, including creating classroom workbooks for elementary students. Tracy's most recently published hard cover book focused on the city of Macon, Georgia. A graduate of the University of Minnesota - Minneapolis School of Journalism, she now lives in Park Falls, Wisconsin, with her husband Mike.

PHOTO CREDITS
© Timothy L. Vacula: cover, title page, pages 8, 12, 17, 18; Courtesy of the American Swedish Institute, Minneapolis, MN: page 4; © Canadian Tourism Commission, Bruce Paton, photographer: page 7; © Lois M. Nelson: page 10; © Michael Le Poer Trench: page 13; © Peter S. Ford: page 15; © Japan National Tourist Organization: page 21

With appreciation to Dr. Jim Rowland, Centerville Fire Department Highland Bagpipe and Drum Band Society, Centerville, GA; Sharona Paller Rubinstein; Lydia McAnerney, Tapestry Folkdance Center, Minneapolis, MN; Merle Frimark Associates, New York, NY, for *Riverdance*

EDITORIAL SERVICES:
Penworthy Learning Systems and Lois M. Nelson

Library of Congress Cataloging-in-Publication Data

Maurer , Tracy, 1965-
    World Dances / Tracy M. Maurer
        p. cm. — (Let's dance)
    Includes index
    Summary: Discusses why and how dance developed as a form of cultural expression and describes dances of various peoples and some of the music, costumes, and instruments involved.
ISBN 1-57103-173-1
    1. Folk dancing—Juvenile literature. 2. Dance—Juvenile literature. 3. Dance—Cross cultural studies—Juvenile literature. [1. Folk dancing. 2. Dance.] I. Title II. Series: Maurer, Tracy, 1965- Let's dance.
GV1596.5.M38 1997
792.3'1—dc21   97-8395
                                                      CIP
                                                      AC

Printed In the USA

TABLE OF CONTENTS

Dance Is Everywhere   5

Why People Dance   6

Where Dances Began   9

Dancing with Props   11

Colorful Costumes   14

A World of Music   16

Learning to Dance   19

It's Fun to Dance   20

Where to See World Dances   22

Glossary   23

Index   24

DANCE IS EVERYWHERE

Dancing is one of the world's oldest arts. Some of the very first people on Earth drew pictures of dances on cave walls.

Most of the world's cultures, or groups of people who share the same ways of living, have created their own dances. Adults and children still perform these **ethnic** (ETH nik) or folk dances.

Each culture's dances usually look very different from one another. The movements, costumes, and music often give clues about the culture's history.

Sweden's maypole dances began hundreds of years ago as part of the June mid-summer festivals.

WHY PEOPLE DANCE

People dance for all kinds of reasons. Many dances began as ways of praying. Others told stories about everyday life, such as planting and harvesting crops. North American Indians used dancing to teach hunting and fighting skills.

Now people dance to learn about their **heritage** (HER i tij) or to learn about other cultures. They also dance to celebrate special events and holidays, such as a wedding or the new year, and just for fun!

6

Today North American Indians, such as those gathered for a powwow at Fort Qu'Appelle in Saskatchewan, Canada, honor their pasts with traditional dances.

WHERE DANCES BEGAN

Folk dances from cold places often use fast footwork in a small area, which works well indoors. Dancers usually move slower in warm **climates** (KLY mits). This helps keep them cool and gives them time to make **expressive** (ik SPRES iv) dance movements.

Many times cultures living along a busy trade route added parts of other cultures' folk dances to their own. Folk dances from areas with few visitors, such as mountain villages, changed very little.

From the northern part of the British Isles, Scotland's joyful Highland dances use complex footwork—and look today much the way they did centuries ago.

9

DANCING WITH PROPS

The fans, torches, and other objects carried by dancers can help tell a story or add excitement to a dance. These props, or properties, may **symbolize** (SIM buh LYZ) part of a dance's history. Baskets in a dance often mean "planting" or "harvesting" in cultures that farm.

Some dancers play small instruments, such as finger cymbals, rattles, or bells that can also tell about the dance's heritage. **Maracas** (muh RAH KUS) appear in dances from the Spanish-speaking cultures of Mexico and Spain.

The Hmong culture remembers its farming heritage in the gestures and props of traditional dances.

Dance schools often teach the dances of other cultures; these dancers hold Spanish castanets, small hand-instruments that click together like little cymbals.

The popular show Riverdance *celebrates the history of Irish dancing and the links between Irish dances and those of other cultures.*

COLORFUL COSTUMES

Nearly every culture has **traditional** (truh DISH uh nul) costumes for its dancers. Japanese women and girls wear kimonos. Russian men and boys wrap wide sashes around their waists.

Sometimes costumes affect the dance. Flowing skirts allow big, fast steps. A tall headdress or a mask can limit a dancer's movement.

The costume may also add sounds to the dancing. The Hawaiian hula dancer's grass skirt makes rustling noises. The American clogger's shoes tap out sounds.

Clogging, an early version of tap dancing, blended European steps to become an American folk dance of the Appalachian mountain area.

A WORLD OF MUSIC

Just about all dancers move to some sort of music. They may make their own music by clapping, stomping, chanting, or singing. Some cultures developed their own instruments, such as the square, guitar-like *shamisen* from Japan. In Scotland, the fancy footwork of a Highland dance would seem odd without **bagpipe** (BAG PYP) music.

Sometimes dancers perform a certain dance with only one song. A dance called the hokey-pokey is done only with the American children's folk song, "Hokey Pokey."

Bagpipers play for many different occasions in Scotland and other countries, but they are especially favored for the famous Scottish Highland dances.

LEARNING TO DANCE

In some countries, folk dances pass from one **generation** (JEN uh RAY shun) to the next without formal lessons.

People of many different cultures moved to the United States during the 1800s. Life in their new country made it difficult for some cultures to keep their folk dances alive.

Today schools, theaters, and community centers work to **preserve** (pri ZERV) these special dances. They offer folk dancing classes to help people learn more about their heritage or to learn more about other cultures.

Some dance schools teach Yiddish dancing, but it is usually passed from one generation to the next without formal lessons.

IT'S FUN TO DANCE

When people dance, they almost always smile. Dancing is fun for everyone of any age!

Most folk dances use simple steps and movements so that everyone in the **community** (kuh MYOO ni tee) can join the dancing. Some countries host huge festivals with dancing in the streets. The *Awa-odori* in Japan highlights one of the most famous of these carnivals.

Even without fancy costumes, folk dancers all over the world can feel linked to their heritage.

About 80,000 people of all ages dance the Awa-odori at the festival held every August in Tokushima, Japan.

WHERE TO SEE WORLD DANCES

The mix of cultures found in big cities has helped to build interest in world dances. Today theaters, schools, and community centers of urban areas host many kinds of dance performances and events such as Kwanza, a celebration of African heritage. Even small towns honor their heritage with lively ethnic festivals.

You can also see world dances on TV programs and videos. Visit the library to learn more about all the special dances of the world.

Glossary

bagpipe (BAG PYP) — a musical instrument often played at dances and ceremonies in Scotland, Ireland, and parts of Europe

climate (KLY mit) — the usual kind of weather for a certain area

community (kuh MYOO ni tee) — a group of people who live in the same area and share the same ways of living

ethnic (ETH nik) — from a group of people who share the same race, language, traditions, or religions

expressive (ik SPRES iv) — meaningful; showing feelings, thoughts, or ideas

generation (JEN uh RAY shun) — all the people alive at the same time; adults form one generation and children form another

heritage (HER i tij) — the history of a group of people

maracas (muh RAH KUS) — gourds with dried seeds or pebbles inside that rattle; gourd-shaped instruments played by shaking

preserve (pri ZERV) — to keep or to save

symbolize (SIM buh LYZ) — to mean something special

traditional (truh DISH uh nul) — an old way; a part of the past

INDEX

bagpipes   16
climates   9
community   20
ethnic   5, 22
expressive   9
folk dances   5, 9, 19
generation   19
heritage   6, 11, 19, 20

hokey pokey   16
instruments   11, 16
maracas   11
preserve   19
props   11
symbolize   11
traditional   14